THEN & NOW

CLIFTON

Opposite: This image exemplifies Clifton's evolving passage from a pastoral, rural town to an energetic, suburban city. The image shown is part of a large mural on an interior wall of the 90-year-old downtown Main Avenue Wachovia bank building. Artist Lauren Smith designed this scene, titled, "The Toll Road, Now Main Avenue Clifton, about 1800," in 1966. (Courtesy of Wachovia Bank, Clifton branch.)

THEN & NOW

CLIFTON

Sandra L. Giordano

In memory of my "Handsome Uncle Tony Tamuzza,"
(January 15, 1946–August 17, 2007), who loved history and art.

Published by Arcadia Publishing
Charleston SC, Chicago IL, Portsmouth NH, San Francisco CA

Printed in the United States of America

For all general information contact Arcadia Publishing at:
Telephone 843-853-2070
Fax 843-853-0044
E-mail sales@arcadiapublishing.com
For customer service and orders:
Toll-Free 1-888-313-2665

Visit us on the Internet at www.arcadiapublishing.com

On the front cover: Depicted is the corner of Clifton and Main Avenues around 1940. It is one of Clifton's busiest and most traversed areas and forms the center of downtown. (Historic photograph courtesy of the Clifton Public Library; contemporary image courtesy of Sandra and Salvatore Giordano.)

On the back cover: Shown here is the Ezorsky family farm, which was located on what today is a senior care facility known as the Daughters of Miriam Home, located on Hazel Street. (Courtesy of the Clifton Public Library.)

Contents

ACKNOWLEDGMENTS

In "a city that cares," it is only fitting to gratefully acknowledge the contributions of the many wonderful angels who made this book possible.

First and foremost, an enormous debt of gratitude is owed to historian Mark S. Auerbach, a most generous man with a heart of gold who is the gatekeeper of history. He shared not only his impressive collection of vintage Clifton images but also his time and expertise.

Many thanks are due also to the following: Roxanne Cammilleri, director of the Clifton Arts Center and Sculpture Park, for her unending encouragement and invaluable support in helping to guide this project; Clifton mayor James Anzaldi for taking an interest in this project and sharing some Clifton history; Cathy Grimshaw and the staff of the Clifton Public Library for providing some scanned images of Clifton's past; and Grandma, Nonna, and Papa for watching my children while I industriously completed this book.

A heartfelt thank you to my wonderful husband, Salvatore, who went with me on many escapades around town and was my photographic partner for several modern Clifton images. A big hug and a thank you go to my children, Christina and Joseph, two young Cliftonites living the history of tomorrow.

And a final thank you goes to the many other individuals who provided photographs, anecdotes, support, advice, and so much more in order to bring this book to fruition. While room does not allow me to fully acknowledge each individual, a most heartfelt thank you is expressed to all.

Unless otherwise noted, all contemporary images are courtesy of Sandra and Salvatore Giordano.

INTRODUCTION

Clifton is a town whose origins date back to the Lenni-Lenape Indians. These peaceful and resourceful Native Americans first inhabited the environs that today form the city of Clifton. In 1684, Dutch settlers purchased this area, which became known as Acquackanonk Township, from the Lenni-Lenape tribe. Much like the Native Americans, the Dutch were attracted to the promising and fertile richness of the land. They came, built homes, and established family farms.

On April 26, 1917, various sections that comprised Acquackanonk Township were separated and Clifton became its own independent city. From then on, more settlers of various origins continued to come and created homes for their families.

Although Clifton has demographically changed and grown over time from a farm town to a commercialized community, it still remains rich in offering resources to its residents. In the past, agricultural resources, including fertile land, open space, and a natural water supply offered opportunities for families to prosper. Today cultural resources, including the area's close proximity to New York City, an arts center that promotes programs for young and old, a nationally-recognized recycling program, a Tree City USA title, the world renowned Clifton Mustang Marching Band, and a recreation department that offers a wealth of activities for families are among the many flourishing factors that continue to make Clifton desirable.

While the face of Clifton may have changed, its roots continue to grow. A deep sense of town pride and community remains constant in the old and new faces that call Clifton home. Be it Botany Village, Dutch Hill, Lakeview, Athenia, Delawanna, Allwood, Richfield, Montclair Heights, or the downtown section of Clifton, residents all over town continue to create a spirit of community that essentially makes Clifton a seasoned hometown with good, old-fashioned values.

Jelaluddin Rumi, a 13th-century mystic poet said, "There is a community of the spirit, join it and feel the delight of walking in the noisy street and being the noise." Turn the pages of Then & Now Clifton to see the joy, hear the noise, and feel the proud spirit both old and new found in the community of Clifton.

CHAPTER 1

CLIFTON ROOTS

Farm peddler Charles Benkendorf is pictured selling farm-fresh produce with his grandchildren happily aboard a vegetable cart. (Courtesy of the Faria family.)

Shown below in this 1952 photograph are Amanda and Rudy Ploch, who are packing produce for market as little Lin Taylor takes a break on top of the truck. Ploch's Farm is Clifton's oldest working farm dating back to the late 1800s when George Ploch, a German settler, established his dairy farm on land extending from Van Houten Avenue to Broad Street. Today Taylor, a fourth-generation descendent, continues the tradition of providing a fresh and rich harvest of the best produce in town. (Historic photograph courtesy of Lin Taylor.)

Many of Clifton's farms originated as dairy farms. One such farm was the Martin Dairy farm situated on what is now part of Weasel Brook Park. Milk was taken as early as 4:00 a.m. in a horse-drawn wagon to be sold around town. To keep milk from spoiling, farmers cut blocks of ice from the Morris Canal in winter, and preserved it amid layers of salt, layers of hay, and sawdust. Blocks of ice were stored in the ice house for use during the summer. (Historic photograph courtesy of the Clifton Public Library.)

The Schwindenhamer farm was situated on the southwest corner of Grove Street and Van Houten Avenue. Farm life in early Clifton was rigorous work. Parents and children would wake at 5:00 a.m. to feed the animals, eat a small breakfast, and continue to work until noon. Then they worked in the field until sundown, ate supper, read the paper, and went to bed by 9:00 p.m. (Historic photograph courtesy of the Clifton Public Library.)

William Hamilton Smith established the Smith farm in 1887 when he moved his family from New York. An old deed cites the property's origin as belonging to Robert Drummond Jr., a noted Acquackanonk Tory who defected to the British in 1776. The farm harvested a bounty of fruits and vegetables, including bushels of tomatoes that were often sold at the roadside by Helen Smith. Parts of the farm's land were sold off as Clifton developed into a suburban city. However, the Smith home remains with family members still living there. (Historic photograph courtesy of the Smith family.)

In 1856, Henry Hamilton purchased a farmhouse and 96 acres of property using profits from his successful milk business. He paid $6,500. This was no small sum at the time. He mortgaged $2,500. The farm was a valuable asset with its rich soil and fertile orchards. One of Hamilton's prized fruits grown on the farm was cantaloupe. (Courtesy of the Hamilton House Museum.)

The above photograph from the late 1880s is the Piaget farm that neighbored the Hamilton farm. The farm encompassed what is today a Gensinger Motors car dealership and extended into the current Route 46 highway situated ar Valley Road and Route 46.

Richfield Farms, located on Van Hauten Avenue, was and still is a family owned and operated working farm. Established in 1917, this farm offered an abundance of crops, including lettuce, carrots, and broccoli. Featured is the original farm stand with the outlying fields in the background. Today Richfield Farms has expanded to include a full-service garden center and nursery where customers can buy an array of products, including paver blocks and freshly-grown vegetables. (Historic photograph courtesy of Deborah Schroeder-Morton.)

Broad Acres, a farm owned by the Benkendorf family, included land along Broad Street as well as land that extended into what is now Route 19. Broad Acres provided a harvest of fruits and vegetables. It was later turned into a florist business. Today the original farm stand building is owned by Dundeee Floor Covering. (Historic photograph courtesy of Mark S. Auerbach.)

Shown here is Wittman's Iris Garden on a postcard from about 1950. Along Van Houten Avenue, directly across from today's Woodrow Wilson Middle School, a lovely, lush bouquet of iris flowers could be purchased. Today the former garden is a parking lot located between a bank and a commercial building. (Historic photograph courtesy of Mark S. Auerbach.)

HOMES AND NEIGHBORHOODS REVISITED

It is said that George Washington visited the home of Clifton's most prominent revolutionary patriot, Henry Garritse, who resided here during the late 1700s. Garritse also owned land now known as Garret Mountain. This house, another prominent example of Dutch Colonial architecture, was demolished in the 1900s. It stood near the northwest corner of Clifton and Lexington Avenues. A gas station has replaced the home. (Courtesy of Mark S. Auerbach.)

Shown here, in a 1941 photograph, is the Van Riper House, which dates back to 1745. It is one of the few Clifton homes built in Federal-style architecture. Originally owned by Philip Van Riper, the house was passed on to his son Adrian, who married and had six children. One child, Catherine, later married William Hamilton from the Hamilton family. The house has been sold several times and additions and renovations have been added. (Historic photograph courtesy of the Clifton Public Library.)

Ancestors of the Van Wagoner and Hamilton families originally inhabited the Hamilton house, a Dutch Colonial, built in 1815. In 1973, the house was turned over to the Clifton Historical Commission and moved to Surgent Park where it stands today. Below is a photograph of the house from the early 1900s. The view is looking north from the kitchen garden and shows a stately flowering English magnolia. Today a condominium complex sits on the former site of the Hamilton home. (Historic photograph courtesy of the Hamilton House Museum.)

On Grove Street, originally called Telegraph Road, is the Smith home, which was built around 1820. The home included a large farm, now a part of Route 46. Although remodeled in the 1950s, original cedar tree trunks hold up the main support beams of the home today. New generations of the Smith family continue to live here. Above is a view of the Smith home as it stands today. (Historic photograph courtesy of the Smith family.)

Described as a "Victorian jewel" and built in 1874 by locally-noted contractor George DeMott, this magnificent home, located on First Street, still looks as impressive today as it did when it was first built. In 1944, the Gutjahr family purchased the home. It is still owned by that family today. (Historic photograph courtesy of the Gutjahr family.)

The Gourley estate, purchased by renowned attorney William B. Gourley in 1888, housed a fine library with many first-edition classics. Gourley was central to establishing Clifton's independence. He famously remarked at a township meeting, "You must adopt or be adopted." Later the home became known as Dolly-Mount Mansion, a small nursing home. Keeping tradition with Gourley's love of the classics, a high-ranking charter school, the Classical Academy, opened at the home in 1998 and continues to provide quality education. (Historic photograph courtesy of Mark S. Auerbach.)

In 1907, when this historic photograph was taken, Passaic Avenue was no more than a dirt road with few houses. It is known today as Harding Avenue. Rumor has it that after the death of Pres. Warren G. Harding in September 1923, Passaic Avenue was renamed in his memory. In the photograph above, note the addition of the modern home built several years later at the corner. (Historic photograph courtesy of Mark S. Auerbach.)

Dr. George Pope, superintendent-veterinarian for the U.S. Department of Agriculture's Quarantine Station, lived in this home with his family. Built in 1901, much of the home's Colonial Revival exterior remains intact today, including the wraparound, columned, wooden porch and the Palladian motif entrance. (Historic photograph courtesy of the Clifton Public Library.)

This Victorian house, dating back to the 1800s, sits at the corner of Second Street and Harding Avenue. Although extensively renovated, it provides hints of its former glory primarily in the third floor, which appears to be in its original state. (Historic photograph courtesy of Mark S. Auerbach.)

Known as the Lindbergh and Hoover Apartments in the 1920s, these buildings along Union Avenue provided comfortable dwellings for a variety of Clifton residents. The apartments remain today. An addition, Union Gardens Condominiums, now occupies what was once a tree-filled lot adjacent to the buildings. (Historic photograph courtesy of Mark S. Auerbach.)

The section of Clifton known as Richfield may very well have acquired its name from the rich harvest of vegetable fields grown in the area by German settlers during the 1800s. Irrigated by the Morris Canal, vegetables, including lettuce, tomatoes, and cauliflower, could be had. In 1948, builder Joseph J. Brunetti developed 108 acres of farmland into garden apartments. The apartments became known as Richfield Village. The complex remains an active dwelling community in Clifton. (Historic photograph courtesy of Mark S. Auerbach.)

This vintage photograph from the late 1930s provides a view of Clifton's residential neighborhood at the corner of Union Avenue and Maple Place. Lou Pounds, who grew up here and still lives on the corner says, "In those days, we had to make our own fun. In spring and summer, we took walks following the Weasel Brook as far as it could take us

into the woods. In winter, we went sleigh riding along Union Ave and in fall, we chased chestnuts from the trees." Children today continue to enjoy walks in the neighborhood. (Historic photograph courtesy of Mark S. Auerbach.)

This 1925 postcard depicts Lakeview Avenue from the corner of Garritse Place. Lakeview Avenue was aptly named because it bordered a lovely lake located near Crooks and Wabash Avenues. Considered a fisherman's delight, it included such wonderful catch as striped bass, pickerel, yellow perch, and catfish. In 1883, the lake was drained, filled, and developed for real estate use. Today a similar neighborhood scene remains visible. (Historic photograph courtesy of Mark S. Auerbach.)

HOMES AND NEIGHBORHOODS REVISITED

DOWNTOWN

This is a watercolor and a pen-and-ink depiction of Sullivan Square in Clifton's Botany Village as it may have looked in 1900. It is by artist Patricia Sprouls. (Courtesy of Mark S. Auerbach.)

The Clifton Grove Hotel, built in the late 1800s on the corner of Madison and Main Avenues, was a wonderful place to dine. Guests enjoyed tasty meals for the modest price of 50¢. In 1895, the hotel burned to the ground. Henry Hohenstein, proprietor, rebuilt it as the Clifton Hotel. Its popularity increased and it remained a landmark until 1942. When the city of Clifton was incorporated in 1917, it functioned as the first city hall. Later a Knights of Columbus hall was built on the site. Today the main Clifton Post Office is situated there. (Historic photograph courtesy of Mark S. Auerbach.)

The original city hall, built in 1914, is still located on the corner of Harding and Main Avenues. Prior to its construction, town meetings, elections, and other city matters were conducted at the Clifton Hotel's reading room. In 1980, city hall relocated to a new building. Today this building is used for commercial purposes and is also the home of the town paper, the *Clifton Journal*. Over time, an addition was built and the stately entrance pillars were removed. (Historic photograph courtesy of Mark S. Auerbach.)

There was no bank in Clifton until 1915 when tax collector S. Grant Thorburn, along with other civic business leaders, founded the Clifton Trust Company. Over $125,000 was deposited on the bank's opening day, May 6, 1915. Over the years, many name changes occurred. Today operating as Wachovia Bank, the bank's exterior remains similar in look to its original design. (Historic photograph courtesy of Mark S. Auerbach.)

John A. Parian was a noted jeweler and optician located on Dayton Avenue in the Botany Village area of Clifton. He began his business in 1921 selling diamonds, gold, and silverware. Three family generations operated the business before it relocated to Franklin Lakes. A travel agency currently occupies the space. (Historic photograph courtesy of Jimmy Marocco.)

Below is Sugarman's drug store around 1920. At this local pharmacy shop, residents could purchase toiletries and greeting cards in addition to prescriptions. The store stood at the southeast corner of Main and Madison Avenues. Today the building has been totally refaced and is home to Koei-Kan Karate, operated by sensei Marco M. Esposito. Awnings continue to embellish the storefronts much like their nostalgic counterparts. (Courtesy of Clifton Public Library.)

POST OFFICE, CLIFTON, N.J.

Between 1870 and 1902, Clifton's post offices provided stamps, money orders, mailboxes, and rural free delivery (RFO). Until 1928 the Cifton Post Office was part of the Passaic Post Office and it operated out of variety stores around town until 1936. It found a home owned by the federal government in a corner building located at Main and Washington Avenues. This building served as the main post office, and later, a branch office. Today's occupant, the recreation department, sponsors a diverse range of activities including a preschool program. (Historic photograph courtesy of Mark S. Auerbach.)

At the beginning of the depression in 1930, Joseph DeLora set out to open a new dry-cleaning business in town called Deluxe Cleaners. Later he designed a unique vaulted room that served as a bomb shelter during World War II and then a fur storage vault. DeLora's ambition proved successful. Over 70 years later, Deluxe Cleaners remains an established family business serving the entire Clifton community. (Historic photograph courtesy of Deluxe Cleaners.)

Located at the southeast corner of Clifton Avenue, the Clifton Theatre, which opened New Year's Day 1937, was the city's largest cinema. It had a seating capacity of 1,100. It operated for over 60 years before it was demolished in 2000 to make room for a Walgreen's pharmacy. (Historic photograph courtesy of Mark S. Auerbach.)

The Marocco Funeral Home, another family-run business, still serves the Botany Village section of town on Parker Avenue. It has provided services to the community for many years. (Historic photograph courtesy of Jimmy Marocco.)

Built in 1924, the grocery shop of Louis and Sophie Wojtan offered a variety of goods, including Hoffman sodas and chicken dinners as advertised in the storefront. The store today has been converted into a single-family home. (Historic photograph courtesy of the Faria family.)

The Alexander Barber Shop was a place "where old friends meet," as the storefront sign advertised. Located on Valley Road, this barbershop offered old-fashioned services to local customers for many years. A modern barbershop is located there today. Next door was the original site of Valley Liquors, which has since relocated to Hazel Street. It is still known to supply "the coldest beer in town!" (Historic photograph courtesy of Ralph Eudice.)

PRAYERFUL PLACES

ORMED CHURCH, ATHENIA, N. J.

Athenia Reformed Church is the oldest continuously operating church in Clifton. It was founded with a worship service on October 6, 1882. In attendance were 19 individuals. At the time, it was called the Reformed Church of Centerville. The photograph above depicts the church built around 1950 in a Colonial Revival design. Located at Clifton Avenue, this church is a reminder of Clifton's religious formations. (Courtesy of Mark S. Auerbach.)

Founded in 1898, Sacred Heart of Jesus Roman Catholic Church was established to serve the needs of Italian-speaking parishioners in the Botany Village area of town. In 1920, a new site was found for the growing parish on the corner of Randolph and Clifton Avenues. The parish continues to thrive today and includes a state-of-the-art elementary school. (Historic photograph courtesy of Mark S. Auerbach.)

SACRED HEART R. C. CHURCH
CLIFTON AND RANDOLPH AVENUES
CLIFTON, N. J.

On Clifton Avenue between First and Second Streets stands St. Peter's, Clifton's first Episcopalian church, built in 1899. A new church was constructed at the same site in 1966. A parish hall and a bell tower were later added. The church continues to provide religious services today, including outreach support missions for homeless families. (Historic photograph courtesy of Mark S. Auerbach.)

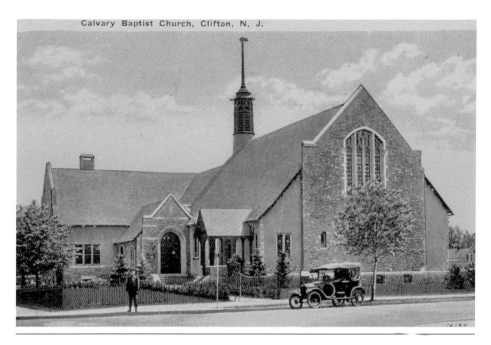

Calvary Baptist Church, Clifton, N. J.

Calvary Baptist Church was organized in 1909. Civic leader and benefactor Samuel Hird generously donated a sizable plot of land on the corner of Lexington and Clifton Avenues in addition to providing $11,000 to secure the church's foundation. This church's beautiful, ornamental facade still remains much the same today as it did when it was built. (Historic photograph courtesy of Mark S. Auerbach.)

PRAYERFUL PLACES

St. Paul's Roman Catholic Church, established in 1913, held its first mass at Clifton Fire Company No. 2's firehouse, which was located on today's Harding Avenue between First and Second Streets. By December 13, 1914, a dedication was held for the church. In 1937, plans for the construction of a new church began. St. Paul's celebrated its 75th anniversary in 1989, and Rev. Msgr. Ronald Amandolare spoke to the congregation, "We reflect and recognize with pride the accomplishments of the founding parishioners, those who have labored to make the dream a reality and those who have nurtured the growth of a new parish." The photograph above depicts the magnificent structure that stands today. (Historic photograph courtesy of Mark S. Auerbach.)

ST. PAVLS R.C. CHVRCH
CLIFTON N.J.

In 1913 SS. Cyril and Methodius Roman Catholic Church was formed for Slovak worshippers in a Clifton firehouse on Arthur Street. A church was built in 1923, as seen in this photograph. Later in 1956, a new church was erected. The original church building is used as an elementary school today. (Historic photograph courtesy of Mark S. Auerbach.)

First Evangelical Lutheran Church was organized in 1925 on the corner of Washington Avenue and Putnam Place. This beautiful Gothic-style church was built to serve many Swedish area residents. In 1966, the congregation relocated to a new church building on Van Houten Avenue. Presently the church is used by Saint Mary's Ukrainian Orthodox congregation. (Historic photograph courtesy of Mark S. Auerbach.)

Trinity Methodist Church, Clifton, N. J.

Trinity United Methodist Church has its original roots in Passaic. The congregation moved to Clifton in 1930 and built a church on DeMott Avenue and Second Street, as depicted in the photograph above. Changes to the structure as seen below have since been made. (Historic photograph courtesy of Mark S. Auerbach.)

Located on Speer Avenue, St. John Kanty was formed to serve Polish-speaking Catholics. Prior to its organization, members traveled to Passaic to hear the mass in Polish. In April 1936, a ground breaking ceremony was held for the creation of a Romanesque-style church. Today the church still serves a strong Polish community. About 40 percent of its parishioners speak Polish at home, and many, much like the founding members, are new immigrants. (Historic photograph courtesy of Mark S. Auerbach.)

Jewish settlers attended religious services in neighboring Passaic or Paterson until 1943 when the Clifton Jewish Center was organized. Finally in 1949, a large building was constructed on the corner of Delaware Street and Barclay Avenue to serve the Jewish community. It continues with Judaic traditions today. (Historic photograph courtesy of Mark S. Auerbach.)

St. George Greek Orthodox Church at 818 Valley Road was built in 1974 and consecrated in 1978. It sits atop a three-acre hill as a majestic replica of an eighth century Greek Byzantine-style basilica built in the shape of a cross and topped with a dome. Today the church offers spiritual guidance to approximately 500 families in Clifton and neighboring communities. (Historic photograph courtesy of St. George Greek Orthodox Church.)

Holy Face Monastery, nestled on top of a mountain off Route 3, remains a popular place for prayer and respite from worldly concerns. Overlooking a majestic skyline view of New York City, the monastery is run by monks who offer a Latin mass on Sundays. Time and technological advances have done little to change its appearance. A lovely stone water fountain in front of the monastery still graces the entrance path. (Historic photograph courtesy of Mark S. Auerbach.)

NEIGHBORHOOD
SCHOOLS

School No. 7 was built on land that is now Randolph Park at Parker Avenue near Ackerman Avenue. It served as both an elementary school and, for a short term, a junior high school before it was torn down in 1965. (Courtesy of Mark S. Auerbach.)

In 1930, a new School No. 1 was built on Park Slope to replace the original School No. 1, which had been located at various prior sites. The school's facade, made to replicate Philadelphia's Independence Hall, was and still is an admirable work of architectural design. Today the school continues to provide elementary instruction to Clifton students. (Historic photograph courtesy of Mark S. Auerbach.)

SCHOOL NO. 1, PARK SLOPE, CLIFTON, N. J.

Neighborhood Schools

Shown above is a vintage postcard depicting School No. 3 in the early 1900s, which was located on the corner of First Street and Clifton Avenue. Presently the school building is home to Pioneer Academy of Science, elementary division, for grades kindergarten through eighth. (Historic photograph courtesy of Mark S. Auerbach.)

School No. 4 was built in the late 1800s on West First Street. On November 27, 1867, the *Paterson Daily Press* reported on the new school, "It is quite large, capable of accommodating one hundred and fifty scholars comfortably . . . This pretty little edifice, one of the most pretentious schoolhouses in the county outside of Paterson, was built by the Acquackanonk town Committee." School No. 4 has since grown with additions. (Historic photograph courtesy of Mark S. Auerbach.)

NEIGHBORHOOD SCHOOLS

In 1912, a new school was needed to house the growing population of elementary students and School No. 5 was constructed on Valley Road. Today, like School No. 4, it has also seen additions to its original structure. (Historic photograph courtesy of the Hamilton House Museum.)

School No. 6 began as a small clapboard school in 1890 on Claverack Road, now known as Clifton Avenue. In 1912, a brick school was built adjacent to the original structure to make room for the increasing student population. Later in 1930, the old wooden schoolhouse was demolished. Today the brick school is home to the Clifton Board of Education. (Historic photograph courtesy of Mark S. Auerbach.)

PUBLIC SCHOOL, ATHENIA, N. J.

School No. 11 on the corner of Merselis and Lakeview Avenues began as a two room, brick schoolhouse amidst pastoral fields in 1907. In 1912, six rooms were added, and by 1926, an additional 16 rooms were constructed. Today the school continues to provide elementary education to a large population of students. (Historic photograph courtesy of Mark S. Auerbach.)

Constructed in 1921 on Van Houten Avenue, School No. 13 serves a large population of students. Note the new additions built in front of the original structure. (Historic photograph courtesy of Mark S. Auerbach.)

Shown below is an old photograph featuring School No. 10, which was located on Clifton Avenue and First Street. It served as an elementary school, a junior high school, and a high school. The first and second floors contained the elementary grades and the third floor served as the high school. In 1964, the school was demolished to make way for a shopper's parking lot that remains today. (Historic photograph courtesy of Mark S. Auerbach.)

High School No. 10, Clifton, N. J.

In the early 1920s, a new high school was built on the land that had previously been home to Clifton's racetrack. The city purchased the land for $100,000. What remained of the land was turned into a park. Later when need arose to construct a larger high school,

NEIGHBORHOOD SCHOOLS

this building was converted to Christopher Columbus Middle School and today houses grades six, seven, and eight. (Historic photograph courtesy of Mark S. Auerbach.)

112   Washington Parochial School, Clifton, N. J.

The Sisters of Charity began a school in the basement of St. Paul's Church in 1916. A year later, they purchased a farmhouse and taught there. By 1922, St. Paul's Parochial School was built to provide a Catholic curriculum for grades kindergarten through eight. In its early years, the school was beautifully landscaped with a verdant lawn. Later blacktop pavement was put in for playground use. After 90 years, the school was closed and the building was leased out to the Pioneer Academy of Science. (Historic photograph courtesy of Mark S. Auerbach.)

CHAPTER

OLD PLACES,
NEW FACES

Opened in May 1905, Fairyland Park was the marvel of its day. Girls dressed in ornate blue and gold attire sold tickets for 10¢ and welcomed visitors at the entrance. But, by 1909, business suddenly declined. The main gates to this enchanting park were closed. Shown above is the entrance to the House of Laughter, a popular attraction in the park. (Courtesy of Mark S. Auerbach.)

Fairyland Park featured rides, including a miniature railway which ran three quarters of a mile through the park, a 1,000-seat theater, a dance pavilion, and the "best of its kind" movie projector. Today the Corrado family has built a food emporium, offering fresh produce and gourmet cheeses. Other businesses on the site include a children's clothing store and a bank. (Historic photograph courtesy of Mark S. Auerbach.)

During winter, children enjoyed skating along Clifton Pond, which was located on the Main Avenue area in downtown Clifton. Currently storefronts and other local businesses preside on what was once the pond. (Historic photograph courtesy of the Clifton Public Library.)

The Erie-Lackawanna Railroad depot operated from 1873 to 1965, serving the Richfield and Athenia area of Clifton at 850 Clifton Avenue. Influenced by the prairie-style with an overhanging, hipped roof, this facade is a notable landmark in town. In 1966, the New Jersey Bank and Trust Company refurbished the station and opened a bank branch. Today Dr. David Moore operates a chiropractic office there, fittingly called On Track Rehabilitation. (Historic photograph courtesy of Mark S. Auerbach.)

OLD PLACES, NEW FACES

One of Clifton's most transformed sites could arguably be what began in 1875 as the Clifton Race Track, a 25-acre horse-racing facility. Although considered the finest in the country, attorney William Gourley led a prosecution against the track. In 1908, it was converted into a velodrome. More changes came in the 1920s when the city purchased the property, creating a park and a new high school, now known as Christopher Columbus Middle School. (Historic photograph courtesy of Mark S. Auerbach.)

The Stadium, Clifton, N.J.

The photograph below features the Henry Doherty Mill and ball field, which was relocated from Paterson to Main Avenue in Clifton in 1908. It was considered the largest silk mill in the United States, employing 1,000 workers. When Henry Doherty Sr.'s son Henry Doherty Jr. took on his father's business, he built the Doherty Oval, where spectators enjoyed watching baseball players for almost 15 years. The oval was considered one of the finest baseball fields including those of the major leagues. Presently several shops are housed in the mill including a shoe store and fabric store. (Historic photograph courtesy of Mark S. Auerbach.)

Athenia Steel Company, Athenia, N.J.

PHOTO BY REGINALD FALK
(5 June 1915)

Athenia Steel Company provided industrial work for residents for many years. Part of it has since been transformed into Senior Horizons, a townhouse community for residents aged 55 and older. (Historic photograph courtesy of Mark S. Auerbach.)

CATTLE BARNS, QUARANTINE, Athenia, N. J.

Shown here are the cattle barns from the United States Animal Quarantine Station, built in 1903. Many prized and exotic animals, including horses, giraffes, antelope, camels, and musk oxen were inspected in the 78 years of the station's operation. In the 1950s, the city began purchasing parts of the land to build a new high school. Below is a picture of the original cattle barns that are in use today as a senior community center and a recycling drop-off center. (Historic photograph courtesy of Mark S. Auerbach.)

OLD PLACES, NEW FACES

In 1966, the city of Clifton purchased an additional 27 acres from the federal government, but was not able to take full possession of the land until 1979 when the U.S. Department of Agriculture relocated the quarantine station to Newburgh, New York. A new city hall complex was constructed on the remaining property in 1980. (Historic photograph courtesy of the Clifton Arts Center.)

Two of the 14 brick barns on the former animal quarantine station were renovated in the 1990s to house the Clifton Arts Center, the city's first multi-arts arena. Above is a photograph from the mid-1980s showing a barn in its original state. Below is a view of the arts center with a newly-designed atrium that connects the gallery barn and studio barn. The atrium, with its large windows and spacious ceiling, is used to welcome visitors

and to host receptions. Clifton Arts Center director Roxanne Cammilleri commented on the center, saying, "Our Clifton residents are equipped not simply with modern technical know how to interact effectively with the community but with opportunities to appreciate our local history." (Historic photograph courtesy of the Clifton Arts Center.)

Many animals, including horses, grazed the green hills of the quarantine station, as seen in the above photograph from the 1970s. It was not uncommon for children to gather along the fence to catch a glimpse of the animals. Cliftonite Lou Pounds said, "As kids, we liked to go to the animal quarantine to see if we could spot any giraffe heads and necks sticking out of the barn roofs!" Today the land serves as a sculpture park, showcasing pieces like the one featured below, *One City One Nation*, by Miklos Sebek. This sculpture represents Clifton's multiculturalism. (Historic photograph courtesy of the Clifton Arts Center.)

OLD PLACES, NEW FACES

Fine food, dancing, and entertainment were readily available at the Penguin Club, whose motto was, "the Country Restaurant with Olde English Charm." It was located on today's Allwood Circle.

Rick's Restaurant and Sports Club, offering more casual entertainment, replaced the Penguin Club. (Historic photograph courtesy of Mark S. Auerbach.)

PENGUIN CLUB INN
ALLWOOD TRAFFIC CIRCLE
CLIFTON, N. J.

The Melody Hill Diner was a great place to grab some good wholesome food. It has since been replaced with franchise eatery, the Boston Market. (Historic photograph courtesy of Mark S. Auerbach.)

America's "first modern strip mall" had its roots in Clifton. The Styretown Shopping Center, designed by developer Albert A. Stier in 1952, featured an assortment of fine stores, including Levy Brothers, Romance Emporium, Bonds Ice Cream, and Wilbur Rogers. Presently stores such as Dress Barn and Kid City offer reasonably-priced merchandise for local shoppers. (Historic photograph courtesy of Mark S. Auerbach.)

In 1946, Shulton, Inc. opened a major manufacturing plant at Colfax Avenue and Route 46. Known for making the famous Old Spice fragrance and other cosmetic toiletries, Shulton provided employment for many residents until it closed its Clifton building in 1991. In 2001, developers Town and Country designed 637 housing units on the property. (Historic photograph courtesy of Mark S. Auerbach.)

CHAPTER 7

HISTORY STILL STANDING

Above is a photograph of some of Clifton's finest civil employees from Clifton Fire Company No. 2.

Located at the intersection of Lexington and Clifton Avenues, Hird Park was created to honor Samuel Hird, a woolen mills magnate and generous benefactor to his community. Upon his death, the *Passaic Daily News* described him as "big in business, big in heart, big in the things of spirit." The park is a welcome haven today for residents to sit and relax in the bustle of downtown Clifton. (Historic photograph courtesy of Mark S. Auerbach.)

Hird Memorial Park. - Clifton N. J.

Shown above is a 1930s photograph of the Clifton Elks lodge, which began with 65 members. The original structure, a lovely Victorian home with a carriage entrance, was located at Colfax and Clifton Avenues. In 1961, the original lodge was destroyed by fire, and a new lodge was built in its stead. The only remaining trace of the original house today is the stone wall that stands directly in front of the lodge. (Historic photograph courtesy of the Clifton Elks lodge.)

The Italian Cooperative hall was built in the early 1920s for the Italian-American Family Association and the Cooperative Grocers. Located at 282 Parker Avenue, it continues to host many local functions and celebrations, much like it did in the past. (Historic photograph courtesy of Jimmy Marocco.)

In 1921, the first library opened in a storefront on Clifton and Madison Avenues with 440 books. By 1950, the library housed 33,000 volumes. On April 16, 1952, ground breaking began for a new library located on Piaget Avenue and Third Street. This photograph features the library around 1953. In 1991, the new Clifton Memorial Library was completed. A dedication ceremony was held in November where the motto, "Door to the Past, Window to the Future," was adopted. Currently the library collection includes over 180,000 books in circulation, along with a 12,000-volume reference collection. Modern features to the library include a computerized card catalog and public use of computer stations with Internet access. (Historic photograph courtesy of Mark S. Auerbach.)

Clifton Fire Station No. 3 was built in 1924 for $50,000. Located at 180 Mahar Avenue, it had the most modern equipment including a 75-foot extension ladder truck and a 700-gallon pumper. It was renovated in 1996 and continues to function as a working firehouse today. (Historic photograph courtesy of Mark S. Auerbach.)

First established in 1948, Tick Tock Diner was and still is an all-time favorite eatery of Clifton residents. Good food and good prices have made it a landmark place to eat. As owner Jimmy Vasipoulos stated in a recent news article feature, "What remains constant at the Tick Tock besides the neon glow of the original Tick Tock sign and famous clock sitting on top of the shiny silver entrance are the customers who make up the atmosphere." (Historic photograph courtesy of Mark S. Auerbach.)

Begun in 1824, the Morris Canal ran along a three-mile stretch through Clifton. Products were shipped along the waterway to markets. The canal also provided many pleasurable amenities, including fishing, swimming, boating, and ice-skating. In 1924, the canal ceased to function. A 600-foot section was resurrected in the 1980s under the direction of Jack Kuepferer, a Clifton resident, who led the effort to create the Morris Canal Park. Pictured at right, a mother and her children enjoy a dip. Below, the author and her children take time to enjoy a piece of Clifton's flowing history.

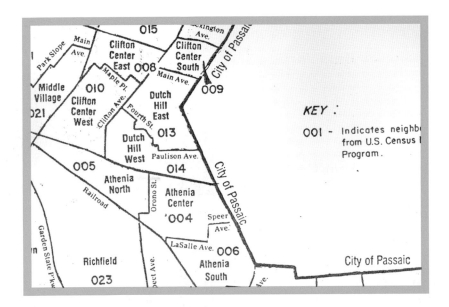

These maps showcase neighborhoods in Clifton both then and now. On April 29, 2007, at Clifton's 90th anniversary dinner, Clifton mayor James Anzaldi said, "We can take pride in Clifton's progress. The solid foundation built by our citizens, government, our schools, businesses, and industries is a reason to look to a continued bright future!"

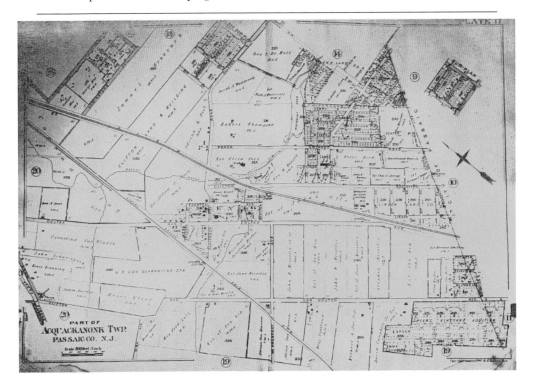

ACROSS AMERICA, PEOPLE ARE DISCOVERING SOMETHING WONDERFUL. *THEIR HERITAGE.*

Arcadia Publishing is the leading local history publisher in the United States. With more than 3,000 titles in print and hundreds of new titles released every year, Arcadia has extensive specialized experience chronicling the history of communities and celebrating America's hidden stories, bringing to life the people, places, and events from the past. To discover the history of other communities across the nation, please visit:

www.arcadiapublishing.com

Customized search tools allow you to find regional history books about the town where you grew up, the cities where your friends and family live, the town where your parents met, or even that retirement spot you've been dreaming about.

MAP SEARCH